LOVE GOD WITH ALL YOUR HEART, MIND, AND SOUL

Retreat/Group Companion
WORKBOOK

RICHARD T. CASE

Dedication/Acknowledgements

I wish to dedicate this course to and thank my wife, Linda, who is a shining example of the joy of living in God's love; and our ministry leaders who have learned this as well. It has been profound to fully understand that we love and can love because He first and does love us. It is a flow through process. He loves us who then invites us to love Him will all our heart mind and soul—and then as we walk together with Him in this love, we are able to extend this love to others, who then learn the same thing; and we all then experience the fullness of God's love—receive, experience and then give away. Linda and the leaders know this love; our marriage is built upon this love and then our ministry community is further built upon this love. It makes the difference between duty, living in judgment & conflict and enjoying the freedom and joy of life as offered by God to us all. Another important element of this love is to receive our instruction from God regarding how we relate to all others without deciding on our own what we think is a good idea. We then fulfill being the extension of His love to the world around us. Thank you, Linda and team. An honor.

These leaders are:
Jake & Mary Beckel
Joe & Leigh Bogar
Heath & Rebecca Cardie
Rich & Janet Cocchiaro
Larry & Sherry Collett
Scott & Kristen Cornell
David & Melissa Dunkel
Tom & Susanne Ewing
Rick & Kelly Ferris
Joel & Christina Gunn
Scott & Terry Hitchcock
Rick & Nancy Hoover
Tad & Monica Jones
Ed & Becky Kobel
Don & Rachelle Light
Chris & Heidi May
Terry & Josephine Noetzel
Towanda Norton
Steve & Carolyn Van Ooteghem
Preston & Lynda Pitts
Dan & Kathy Rocconi
Bob & Keri Rockwell
John & Michelle Santaferraro
Allyson & Denny Weinberg
Neal & Kathy Weisenburger

LOVE GOD WITH ALL YOUR HEART, MIND, AND SOUL COMPANION WORKBOOK
PUBLISHED BY LIVING WATERS—ABIDE MINISTRIES
7615 Lemon Gulch Way
Castle Rock, CO 80108

Unless otherwise noted, all Scripture quotations are from the ESV® Bible (The Holy Bible, English Standard Version®), copyright © 2001 by Crossway Bibles, a publishing ministry of Good News Publishers. Used by permission. All rights reserved.

ISBN: 979-8-218-14831-7
Copyright © 2024 by Richard T. Case.

All rights reserved. No part of this publication may be reproduced, distributed or transmitted in any form or by any means, including photocopying, recording, or other electronic or mechanical methods, without the prior written permission of the publisher.

Publisher's Cataloging-in-Publication data

Names:
Title:
Description: .
Identifiers: ISBN | LCCN
Subjects:

Printed in the United States of America 2023 — 2nd ed

TABLE OF CONTENTS

Lesson One:
What Is God's Love & What Does It Mean in a World of Difficulty
As God Restores Us From This World?. 2

Lesson Two:
What Are Elements of His Love That We Will Experience if We Walk With Him?. 16

Lesson Three:
How Does God's Love Lead Us to His Good, Best and Supernatural Life for Us?. 34

Lesson Four:
What Are the Conditions of Living In and Receiving God's Love
That Provides Wonderful Aspects of the Fullness of God's Life?. 50

Lesson Five:
How Do We Love Others and Help Them To Learn To Love God With All Their Heart?. 60

LESSON 1:
WHAT IS GOD'S LOVE & WHAT DOES IT MEAN IN A WORLD OF DIFFICULTY AS GOD RESTORES US FROM THIS WORLD?

From the following verses, write out the definition of love. How has God loved us? Why is that love? What does this mean for us to understand love and receive love?

> **Read 1 John 4:7–11:**
>
> God Is Love
> ⁷ Beloved, let us love one another, for love is from God, and whoever loves has been born of God and knows God. ⁸ Anyone who does not love does not know God, because God is love. ⁹ In this the love of God was made manifest among us, that God sent his only Son into the world, so that we might live through him. ¹⁰ In this is love, not that we have loved God but that he loved us and sent his Son to be the propitiation for our sins. ¹¹ Beloved, if God so loved us, we also ought to love one another.

"It says we know God because God IS LOVE; and this love of God was made to manifest among us by God sending His only Son into the world so that we might live through Him."

_____
_____
_____
_____
_____
_____
_____

LESSON 1:
WHAT IS GOD'S LOVE & WHAT DOES IT MEAN IN A WORLD OF DIFFICULTY AS GOD RESTORES US FROM THIS WORLD?

What does this verse say about who we are if we receive His love? What does that mean? Think of the benefits of being a child of the King. How is this love toward us to be received by us?

> **Read 1 John 3:1:**
>
> **3** See what kind of love the Father has given to us, that we should be called children of God; and so we are. The reason why the world does not know us is that it did not know him.

_____
_____
_____
_____
_____

In Genesis 1 and 2, before the fall, He gave us exceptional authority—victory and power over life, and we were to be a co-creator with Him, exercising the authority over His creation—over the Earth and over the things of the Earth.

In the following four sets of verses, what do we see are the benefits of the exceptional life He has planned for us as recipients of His love? Why is each so important to how we view this planned life and are able to experience this love?

> **Read Genesis 1:1–3:**
>
> The Creation of the World
> ¹ In the beginning, God created the heavens and the earth. ² The earth was without form and void, and darkness was over the face of the deep. And the Spirit of God was hovering over the face of the waters.
>
> ³ And God said, "Let there be light," and there was light.

LESSON 1:
WHAT IS GOD'S LOVE & WHAT DOES IT MEAN IN A WORLD OF DIFFICULTY AS GOD RESTORES US FROM THIS WORLD?

> **Read Genesis 1:26–27:**
>
> 26 Then God said, "Let us make man[a] in our image, after our likeness. And let them have dominion over the fish of the sea and over the birds of the heavens and over the livestock and over all the earth and over every creeping thing that creeps on the earth."
>
> 27 So God created man in his own image,
> in the image of God he created him;
> male and female he created them.

> **Read Genesis 2:15:**
>
> 15 The LORD God took the man and put him in the garden of Eden to work it and keep it.

LESSON 1:
WHAT IS GOD'S LOVE & WHAT DOES IT MEAN IN A WORLD OF DIFFICULTY AS GOD RESTORES US FROM THIS WORLD?

> **Read Genesis 2:18–25:**
>
> [18] Then the LORD God said, "It is not good that the man should be alone; I will make him a helper fit for[a] him." [19] Now out of the ground the LORD God had formed[b] every beast of the field and every bird of the heavens and brought them to the man to see what he would call them. And whatever the man called every living creature, that was its name. [20] The man gave names to all livestock and to the birds of the heavens and to every beast of the field. But for Adam[c] there was not found a helper fit for him. [21] So the LORD God caused a deep sleep to fall upon the man, and while he slept took one of his ribs and closed up its place with flesh. [22] And the rib that the LORD God had taken from the man he made[d] into a woman and brought her to the man. [23] Then the man said,
>
> "This at last is bone of my bones
>   and flesh of my flesh;
> she shall be called Woman,
>   because she was taken out of Man."[e]
>
> [24] Therefore a man shall leave his father and his mother and hold fast to his wife, and they shall become one flesh. [25] And the man and his wife were both naked and were not ashamed.

_____

_____

_____

_____

LESSON 1:
WHAT IS GOD'S LOVE & WHAT DOES IT MEAN IN A WORLD OF DIFFICULTY AS GOD RESTORES US FROM THIS WORLD?

As we are called to oneness, what is the benefit of going to unity with our spouse, with our friends, with our inner circle? What is the significance of this?

> **Read Psalm 133:**
>
> When Brothers Dwell in Unity
> A Song of Ascents. Of David.
>
> **133** Behold, how good and pleasant it is
>   when brothers dwell in unity![a]
> [2] It is like the precious oil on the head,
>   running down on the beard,
> on the beard of Aaron,
>   running down on the collar of his robes!
> [3] It is like the dew of Hermon,
>   which falls on the mountains of Zion!
> For there the LORD has commanded the blessing,
>   life forevermore.

_____
_____
_____
_____
_____

In Christ's temptation, what did Satan offer? Who gave him this authority of the kingdoms on Earth? What does that imply, and why is that important to us?

> **Read Luke 4:5–8:**
>
> [5] And the devil took him up and showed him all the kingdoms of the world in a moment of time, 6 and said to him, "To you I will give all this authority and their glory, for it has been delivered to me, and I give it to whom I will. [7] If you, then, will worship me, it will all be yours." [8] And Jesus answered him, "It is written,
>
> "'You shall worship the Lord your God,
>   and him only shall you serve.'"

LESSON 1:
WHAT IS GOD'S LOVE & WHAT DOES IT MEAN IN A WORLD OF DIFFICULTY AS GOD RESTORES US FROM THIS WORLD?

_____
_____
_____
_____
_____

Because of the sin nature of all humans on Earth, what is the consequence of our ability to have a relationship with God? Why? How was God's remedy to the problem an act of love? To receive this love, what is required now by us? What happens when we meet this requirement?

> **Read John 3:16–18:**
>
> For God So Loved the World
>
> [16] "For God so loved the world,[a] that he gave his only Son, that whoever believes in him should not perish but have eternal life. [17] For God did not send his Son into the world to condemn the world, but in order that the world might be saved through him. [18] Whoever believes in him is not condemned, but whoever does not believe is condemned already, because he has not believed in the name of the only Son of God.

_____
_____
_____
_____
_____

LESSON 1:
WHAT IS GOD'S LOVE & WHAT DOES IT MEAN IN A WORLD OF DIFFICULTY AS GOD RESTORES US FROM THIS WORLD?

After the resurrection, what is still true about Satan's control—authority and dominion—over the world? What does that mean for all of us—even believers—today?

> **Read 1 John 5:18–20:**
>
> [18] We know that everyone who has been born of God does not keep on sinning, but he who was born of God protects him, and the evil one does not touch him. [19] We know that we are from God, and the whole world lies in the power of the evil one.
>
> [20] And we know that the Son of God has come and has given us understanding, so that we may know him who is true; and we are in him who is true, in his Son Jesus Christ. He is the true God and eternal life.

_____
_____
_____
_____
_____

Despite the control of the enemy on Earth, what has God done that we might still experience His love? On what basis did He fulfill this? What then does this mean for how we are to live?

> **Read 1 John 4:7–11:**
>
> God Is Love
>
> [7] Beloved, let us love one another, for love is from God, and whoever loves has been born of God and knows God. [8] Anyone who does not love does not know God, because God is love. [9] In this the love of God was made manifest among us, that God sent his only Son into the world, so that we might live through him. [10] In this is love, not that we have loved God but that he loved us and sent his Son to be the propitiation for our sins. [11] Beloved, if God so loved us, we also ought to love one another.

LESSON 1:
WHAT IS GOD'S LOVE & WHAT DOES IT MEAN IN A WORLD OF DIFFICULTY AS GOD RESTORES US FROM THIS WORLD?

_____
_____
_____
_____
_____

As we revisit these verses, what is the choice that has to be made in order to have life with God? Why? What does this then imply for how we are to live?

> **Read John 3:16–19:**
>
> For God So Loved the World
>
> [16] "For God so loved the world,[a] that he gave his only Son, that whoever believes in him should not perish but have eternal life. [17] For God did not send his Son into the world to condemn the world, but in order that the world might be saved through him. [18] Whoever believes in him is not condemned, but whoever does not believe is condemned already, because he has not believed in the name of the only Son of God. [19] And this is the judgment: the light has come into the world, and people loved the darkness rather than the light because their works were evil.

_____
_____
_____
_____
_____

LESSON 1:
WHAT IS GOD'S LOVE & WHAT DOES IT MEAN IN A WORLD OF DIFFICULTY AS GOD RESTORES US FROM THIS WORLD?

What is the reason that Jesus could not do miracles in Nazareth? What does that imply then for how we are to live to experience the fullness of the life of God and His supernatural work in and for our lives?

> **Read Mark 6:1–6:**
>
> Jesus Rejected at Nazareth
> **6** He went away from there and came to his hometown, and his disciples followed him. ² And on the Sabbath he began to teach in the synagogue, and many who heard him were astonished, saying, "Where did this man get these things? What is the wisdom given to him? How are such mighty works done by his hands? ³ Is not this the carpenter, the son of Mary and brother of James and Joses and Judas and Simon? And are not his sisters here with us?" And they took offense at him. ⁴ And Jesus said to them, "A prophet is not without honor, except in his hometown and among his relatives and in his own household." ⁵ And he could do no mighty work there, except that he laid his hands on a few sick people and healed them. ⁶ And he marveled because of their unbelief.
>
> And he went about among the villages teaching.

_____
_____
_____
_____
_____

LESSON 1:
WHAT IS GOD'S LOVE & WHAT DOES IT MEAN IN A WORLD OF DIFFICULTY AS GOD RESTORES US FROM THIS WORLD?

What are the two consequences of us establishing and living by law (rules) that attempt to provide our own way of spiritual living? What does that mean for us and the choice we must make to live the true, supernatural life of God?

> **Read Galatians 5:1–4:**
>
> Christ Has Set Us Free
> **5** For freedom Christ has set us free; stand firm therefore, and do not submit again to a yoke of slavery.
>
> ² Look: I, Paul, say to you that if you accept circumcision, Christ will be of no advantage to you. ³ I testify again to every man who accepts circumcision that he is obligated to keep the whole law. ⁴ You are severed from Christ, you who would be justified[a] by the law; you have fallen away from grace.

_____
_____
_____
_____
_____

LESSON 1:
WHAT IS GOD'S LOVE & WHAT DOES IT MEAN IN A WORLD OF DIFFICULTY AS GOD RESTORES US FROM THIS WORLD?

What determines our "reward" in heaven? What thus are the two possibilities regarding the way we live our life? Based upon what? How important is it for how we live our life now? Why?

> **Read 1 Corinthians 3:9–15:**
>
> ⁹ For we are God's fellow workers. You are God's field, God's building. ¹⁰ According to the grace of God given to me, like a skilled[a] master builder I laid a foundation, and someone else is building upon it. Let each one take care how he builds upon it. ¹¹ For no one can lay a foundation other than that which is laid, which is Jesus Christ. ¹² Now if anyone builds on the foundation with gold, silver, precious stones, wood, hay, straw— ¹³ each one's work will become manifest, for the Day will disclose it, because it will be revealed by fire, and the fire will test what sort of work each one has done. ¹⁴ If the work that anyone has built on the foundation survives, he will receive a reward. ¹⁵ If anyone's work is burned up, he will suffer loss, though he himself will be saved, but only as through fire.

_____
_____
_____
_____
_____

Even though we may not choose to walk with Him and receive His love, what is always true? Why is this so significant for us? What is the good news about this?

> **Read Hebrews 13:5:**
>
> ⁵ Keep your life free from love of money, and be content with what you have, for he has said, "I will never leave you nor forsake you."

LESSON 1:
WHAT IS GOD'S LOVE & WHAT DOES IT MEAN IN A WORLD OF DIFFICULTY AS GOD RESTORES US FROM THIS WORLD?

_____
_____
_____
_____
_____

What was the relationship with the Israelites who refused to enter the Promised Land and follow God? Why were they not then able to enter the Promised Land? Why was entering the Promised Land not automatic as children of God? What is the implication for how we are to live?

Read Hebrews 3:15–19:

¹⁵ As it is said,

"Today, if you hear his voice,
do not harden your hearts as in the rebellion."

¹⁶ For who were those who heard and yet rebelled? Was it not all those who left Egypt led by Moses? ¹⁷ And with whom was he provoked for forty years? Was it not with those who sinned, whose bodies fell in the wilderness? ¹⁸ And to whom did he swear that they would not enter his rest, but to those who were disobedient? ¹⁹ So we see that they were unable to enter because of unbelief.

_____
_____
_____
_____
_____

LESSON 1:
WHAT IS GOD'S LOVE & WHAT DOES IT MEAN IN A WORLD OF DIFFICULTY AS GOD RESTORES US FROM THIS WORLD?

As we understand the consequences of not choosing to follow God, how are we to follow God? What happens when we do, and why is this so important to our experience of His life in and through us?

Read Romans 8:5; 9–17:

5 For those who live according to the flesh set their minds on the things of the flesh, but those who live according to the Spirit set their minds on the things of the Spirit.

9 You, however, are not in the flesh but in the Spirit, if in fact the Spirit of God dwells in you. Anyone who does not have the Spirit of Christ does not belong to him. 10 But if Christ is in you, although the body is dead because of sin, the Spirit is life because of righteousness. 11 If the Spirit of him who raised Jesus from the dead dwells in you, he who raised Christ Jesus[a] from the dead will also give life to your mortal bodies through his Spirit who dwells in you.

Heirs with Christ
12 So then, brothers,[b] we are debtors, not to the flesh, to live according to the flesh. 13 For if you live according to the flesh you will die, but if by the Spirit you put to death the deeds of the body, you will live. 14 For all who are led by the Spirit of God are sons[c] of God. 15 For you did not receive the spirit of slavery to fall back into fear, but you have received the Spirit of adoption as sons, by whom we cry, "Abba! Father!" 16 The Spirit himself bears witness with our spirit that we are children of God, 17 and if children, then heirs—heirs of God and fellow heirs with Christ, provided we suffer with him in order that we may also be glorified with him.

_____
_____
_____
_____
_____

LESSON 1:
WHAT IS GOD'S LOVE & WHAT DOES IT MEAN IN A WORLD OF DIFFICULTY AS GOD RESTORES US FROM THIS WORLD?

What will we discover when we choose to follow God? What will that mean to how we live and experience the life of God?

> **Read Ephesians 5:17–21:**
>
> [17] Therefore do not be foolish, but understand what the will of the Lord is. [18] And do not get drunk with wine, for that is debauchery, but be filled with the Spirit, [19] addressing one another in psalms and hymns and spiritual songs, singing and making melody to the Lord with your heart, [20] giving thanks always and for everything to God the Father in the name of our Lord Jesus Christ, [21] submitting to one another out of reverence for Christ.

_____
_____
_____
_____
_____

What is another benefit of choosing to follow God? What does that mean to experience His life for us?

> **Read 1 John 5:3–5:**
>
> [3] For this is the love of God, that we keep his commandments. And his commandments are not burdensome. [4] For everyone who has been born of God overcomes the world. And this is the victory that has overcome the world—our faith. [5] Who is it that overcomes the world except the one who believes that Jesus is the Son of God?

_____
_____
_____
_____
_____

LESSON 2:
WHAT ARE ELEMENTS OF HIS LOVE THAT WE WILL EXPEREINCE IF WE WALK WITH HIM?

"God created us (men and women) in His image, and we are called to be the visible expression of the invisible God—to live out the life that He planned originally."

How did Jesus define eternal life? What does that mean to our experience of life here? Why?

Read John 17:3:

3 And this is eternal life, that they know you, the only true God, and Jesus Christ whom you have sent.

_____
_____
_____
_____

As we experience this eternal life here and now, what will we receive? What does that mean for our experience in this life? Why?

Read 2 Peter 1:1–4:

Greeting
1 Simeon[a] Peter, a servant[b] and apostle of Jesus Christ,

To those who have obtained a faith of equal standing with ours by the righteousness of our God and Savior Jesus Christ:

2 May grace and peace be multiplied to you in the knowledge of God and of Jesus our Lord.
Confirm Your Calling and Election
3 His divine power has granted to us all things that pertain to life and godliness, through the knowledge of him who called us to[c] his own glory and excellence,[d] 4 by which he has granted to us his precious and very great promises, so that through them you may become partakers of the divine nature, having escaped from the corruption that is in the world because of sinful desire.

LESSON 2:
WHAT ARE ELEMENTS OF HIS LOVE THAT WE WILL EXPEREINCE IF WE WALK WITH HIM?

_____
_____
_____
_____
_____

On what basis will we receive His divine nature to live life? What is important to receive this and why?

> **Read Deuteronomy 7:6–9:**
>
> [6] "For you are a people holy to the LORD your God. The LORD your God has chosen you to be a people for his treasured possession, out of all the peoples who are on the face of the earth. [7] It was not because you were more in number than any other people that the LORD set his love on you and chose you, for you were the fewest of all peoples, [8] but it is because the Lord loves you and is keeping the oath that he swore to your fathers, that the Lord has brought you out with a mighty hand and redeemed you from the house of slavery, from the hand of Pharaoh king of Egypt. [9] Know therefore that the LORD your God is God, the faithful God who keeps covenant and steadfast love with those who love him and keep his commandments, to a thousand generations,

_____
_____
_____
_____
_____

LESSON 2:
WHAT ARE ELEMENTS OF HIS LOVE THAT WE WILL EXPEREINCE IF WE WALK WITH HIM?

In addition to us being individual followers of Christ, what is an essential part of God's exceptional life for us? Why is this so important? What does that mean for how we live?

Read Genesis 2:18–25:

[18] Then the LORD God said, "It is not good that the man should be alone; I will make him a helper fit for[a] him." [19] Now out of the ground the LORD God had formed[b] every beast of the field and every bird of the heavens and brought them to the man to see what he would call them. And whatever the man called every living creature, that was its name. [20] The man gave names to all livestock and to the birds of the heavens and to every beast of the field. But for Adam[c] there was not found a helper fit for him. [21] So the LORD God caused a deep sleep to fall upon the man, and while he slept took one of his ribs and closed up its place with flesh. [22] And the rib that the LORD God had taken from the man he made[d] into a woman and brought her to the man. [23] Then the man said,

"This at last is bone of my bones
    and flesh of my flesh;
she shall be called Woman,
    because she was taken out of Man."[e]

[24] Therefore a man shall leave his father and his mother and hold fast to his wife, and they shall become one flesh. [25] And the man and his wife were both naked and were not ashamed.

_____
_____
_____
_____
_____

LESSON 2:
WHAT ARE ELEMENTS OF HIS LOVE THAT WE WILL EXPEREINCE IF WE WALK WITH HIM?

How does God define the elements of His exceptional life for us? How do we live this out? What will we experience if we do?

Read Psalm 128:1–6:

Blessed Is Everyone Who Fears the LORD
A Song of Ascents.
128 Blessed is everyone who fears the LORD,
   who walks in his ways!
² You shall eat the fruit of the labor of your hands;
   you shall be blessed, and it shall be well with you.
³ Your wife will be like a fruitful vine
   within your house;
your children will be like olive shoots
   around your table.
⁴ Behold, thus shall the man be blessed
   who fears the LORD.
⁵ The LORD bless you from Zion!
   May you see the prosperity of Jerusalem
   all the days of your life!
⁶ May you see your children's children!
   Peace be upon Israel!

_____
_____
_____
_____
_____

LESSON 2:
WHAT ARE ELEMENTS OF HIS LOVE THAT WE WILL EXPEREINCE IF WE WALK WITH HIM?

If we are to enjoy sweet fellowship, what is essential about our fellowship? What is important then for how we live in fellowship? Why?

> **Read 1 Corinthians 1:10:**
>
> Divisions in the Church
> 10 I appeal to you, brothers,[a] by the name of our Lord Jesus Christ, that all of you agree, and that there be no divisions among you, but that you be united in the same mind and the same judgment.

_____
_____
_____
_____
_____

Define a joyful life. How do we live a joyful life? What does that mean in how we live this out?

> **Read Psalm 100:1–5:**
>
> His Steadfast Love Endures Forever
> A Psalm for giving thanks.
> **100** Make a joyful noise to the Lord, all the earth!
> 2 Serve the LORD with gladness!
>   Come into his presence with singing!
> 3 Know that the LORD, he is God!
>   It is he who made us, and we are his;[a]
>   we are his people, and the sheep of his pasture.
> 4 Enter his gates with thanksgiving,
>   and his courts with praise!
>   Give thanks to him; bless his name!
> 5 For the LORD is good;
>   his steadfast love endures forever,
>   and his faithfulness to all generations.

LESSON 2:
WHAT ARE ELEMENTS OF HIS LOVE THAT WE WILL EXPEREINCE IF WE WALK WITH HIM?

_____
_____
_____
_____
_____

We can live a joyful life because of what? What does that mean for how we receive this and experience joy?

> **Read Psalm 149:1–5:**
>
> Sing to the LORD a New Song
> **149** Praise the Lord!
> Sing to the LORD a new song,
>   his praise in the assembly of the godly!
> ² Let Israel be glad in his Maker;
>   let the children of Zion rejoice in their King!
> ³ Let them praise his name with dancing,
>   making melody to him with tambourine and lyre!
> ⁴ For the LORD takes pleasure in his people;
>   he adorns the humble with salvation.
> ⁵ Let the godly exult in glory;
>   let them sing for joy on their beds.

_____
_____
_____
_____
_____

LESSON 2:
WHAT ARE ELEMENTS OF HIS LOVE THAT WE WILL EXPEREINCE IF WE WALK WITH HIM?

If we live this joyful life, what is one of the significant benefits of this? What then does this mean to how we live out life?

> **Read Zephaniah 3:14–17:**
>
> Israel's Joy and Restoration
> ¹⁴ Sing aloud, O daughter of Zion;
>   shout, O Israel!
> Rejoice and exult with all your heart,
>   O daughter of Jerusalem!
> ¹⁵ The LORD has taken away the judgments against you;
>   he has cleared away your enemies.
> The King of Israel, the Lord, is in your midst;
>   you shall never again fear evil.
> ¹⁶ On that day it shall be said to Jerusalem:
> "Fear not, O Zion;
>   let not your hands grow weak.
> ¹⁷ The LORD your God is in your midst,
>   a mighty one who will save;
> he will rejoice over you with gladness;
>   he will quiet you by his love;
> he will exult over you with loud singing.

_____
_____
_____
_____
_____

LESSON 2:
WHAT ARE ELEMENTS OF HIS LOVE THAT WE WILL EXPEREINCE IF WE WALK WITH HIM?

In the following three sets of verses, what are the elements of living a joyful life? How might we then practically live this way?

Read Ecclesiastes 5:18–20:

[18] Behold, what I have seen to be good and fitting is to eat and drink and find enjoyment[a] in all the toil with which one toils under the sun the few days of his life that God has given him, for this is his lot. [19] Everyone also to whom God has given wealth and possessions and power to enjoy them, and to accept his lot and rejoice in his toil—this is the gift of God. [20] For he will not much remember the days of his life because God keeps him occupied with joy in his heart.

_____
_____
_____
_____
_____

Read Ecclesiastes 2:24–25:

[24] There is nothing better for a person than that he should eat and drink and find enjoyment[a] in his toil. This also, I saw, is from the hand of God, [25] for apart from him[b] who can eat or who can have enjoyment?

_____
_____
_____
_____
_____

LESSON 2:
WHAT ARE ELEMENTS OF HIS LOVE THAT WE WILL EXPEREINCE IF WE WALK WITH HIM?

> **Read Ecclesiastes 3:12–13:**
>
> [12] I perceived that there is nothing better for them than to be joyful and to do good as long as they live; [13] also that everyone should eat and drink and take pleasure in all his toil—this is God's gift to man.

_____
_____
_____
_____

What is the difference between working to achieve the joyful life versus receiving it from God, who loves us? Why is this important?

> **Read 1 Timothy 6:17:**
>
> [17] As for the rich in this present age, charge them not to be haughty, nor to set their hopes on the uncertainty of riches, but on God, who richly provides us with everything to enjoy.

_____
_____
_____
_____
_____

LESSON 2:
WHAT ARE ELEMENTS OF HIS LOVE THAT WE WILL EXPEREINCE IF WE WALK WITH HIM?

What should characterize your life? How might we experience that in our everyday lives?

> **Read Psalm 126:2–3:**
>
> ² Then our mouth was filled with laughter,
>   and our tongue with shouts of joy;
> then they said among the nations,
>   "The LORD has done great things for them."
> ³ The LORD has done great things for us;
>   we are glad.

_____
_____
_____
_____
_____

As we walk in the Spirit, what will we experience? When? What does that mean then for us?

> **Read 2 Corinthians 3:17:**
>
> ¹⁷ Now the Lord[a] is the Spirit, and where the Spirit of the Lord is, there is freedom.

_____
_____
_____
_____
_____

LESSON 2:
WHAT ARE ELEMENTS OF HIS LOVE THAT WE WILL EXPEREINCE IF WE WALK WITH HIM?

As we walk in the Spirit, we will be given the Covenant—God's promise to all of us who walk with Him. What is the Covenant? What does that mean as far as what we are to expect in how we live in our relationship with receiving God's love?

Read Genesis 12:1–3:

The Call of Abram
12 Now the LORD said[a] to Abram, "Go from your country[b] and your kindred and your father's house to the land that I will show you. ² And I will make of you a great nation, and I will bless you and make your name great, so that you will be a blessing. ³ I will bless those who bless you, and him who dishonors you I will curse, and in you all the families of the earth shall be blessed."[c]

_____
_____
_____
_____
_____

What are all the benefits of living in the Covenant? What does that mean for how we are to live?

Read Psalm 111:

Great Are the Lord's Works
111 [a] Praise the LORD!
I will give thanks to the LORD with my whole heart,
　　in the company of the upright, in the congregation.
² Great are the works of the LORD,
　　studied by all who delight in them.
³ Full of splendor and majesty is his work,
　　and his righteousness endures forever.

LESSON 2:
WHAT ARE ELEMENTS OF HIS LOVE THAT WE WILL EXPEREINCE IF WE WALK WITH HIM?

> 4 He has caused his wondrous works to be remembered;
>   the Lord is gracious and merciful.
> 5 He provides food for those who fear him;
>   he remembers his covenant forever.
> 6 He has shown his people the power of his works,
>   in giving them the inheritance of the nations.
> 7 The works of his hands are faithful and just;
>   all his precepts are trustworthy;
> 8 they are established forever and ever,
>   to be performed with faithfulness and uprightness.
> 9 He sent redemption to his people;
>   he has commanded his covenant forever.
>   Holy and awesome is his name!
> 10 The fear of the LORD is the beginning of wisdom;
>   all those who practice it have a good understanding.
>   His praise endures forever!

_____
_____
_____
_____
_____

To whom was the Covenant given? Why is this important then for how we are to receive the Covenant?

> **Read Galatians 3:15–18; 26–29:**
>
> The Law and the Promise
> 15 To give a human example, brothers:[a] even with a man-made covenant, no one annuls it or adds to it once it has been ratified. 16 Now the promises were made to Abraham and to his offspring. It does not say, "And to offsprings," referring to many, but referring to one, "And to your offspring," who is

LESSON 2:
WHAT ARE THE DIFFERENT ELEMENTS OF GOD PROVIDING OVERCOMING AND DELIVERANCE?

> Christ. [17] This is what I mean: the law, which came 430 years afterward, does not annul a covenant previously ratified by God, so as to make the promise void. [18] For if the inheritance comes by the law, it no longer comes by promise; but God gave it to Abraham by a promise.
>
> [26] for in Christ Jesus you are all sons of God, through faith. [27] For as many of you as were baptized into Christ have put on Christ. [28] There is neither Jew nor Greek, there is neither slave[a] nor free, there is no male and female, for you are all one in Christ Jesus. [29] And if you are Christ's, then you are Abraham's offspring, heirs according to promise.

_____
_____
_____
_____
_____

If we are living in Christ, following Him as shepherd, what will be true of all the days of our lives? What does this mean then for the type of life we experience?

> **Read Psalm 23:6:**
>
> [6] Surely[a] goodness and mercy[b] shall follow me
>   all the days of my life,
> and I shall dwell[c] in the house of the Lord
>   forever.[d]

_____
_____
_____
_____
_____

LESSON 2:
WHAT ARE THE DIFFERENT ELEMENTS OF GOD PROVIDING OVERCOMING AND DELIVERANCE?

What does God promise to those who are following Him? How do we play this out then as we imagine our life?

> **Read Ephesians 3:15–21:**
>
> [15] from whom every family[a] in heaven and on earth is named, [16] that according to the riches of his glory he may grant you to be strengthened with power through his Spirit in your inner being, [17] so that Christ may dwell in your hearts through faith—that you, being rooted and grounded in love, [18] may have strength to comprehend with all the saints what is the breadth and length and height and depth, [19] and to know the love of Christ that surpasses knowledge, that you may be filled with all the fullness of God.
>
> [20] Now to him who is able to do far more abundantly than all that we ask or think, according to the power at work within us, [21] to him be glory in the church and in Christ Jesus throughout all generations, forever and ever. Amen.

_____
_____
_____
_____
_____

LESSON 2:
WHAT ARE ELEMENTS OF HIS LOVE THAT WE WILL EXPEREINCE IF WE WALK WITH HIM?

What does it mean to not neglect so great a salvation? If we do experience God's full salvation for us, what will God demonstrate in our life? What does that mean regarding how we are to live?

> **Read Hebrews 2:1–4:**
>
> Warning Against Neglecting Salvation
> **2** Therefore we must pay much closer attention to what we have heard, lest we drift away from it. ² For since the message declared by angels proved to be reliable, and every transgression or disobedience received a just retribution, ³ how shall we escape if we neglect such a great salvation? It was declared at first by the Lord, and it was attested to us by those who heard, ⁴ while God also bore witness by signs and wonders and various miracles and by gifts of the Holy Spirit distributed according to his will.

_____
_____
_____
_____
_____

As we are living the supernatural life of God, what else will we receive? Why is that so important to us?

> **Read Proverbs 8: 7–18:**
>
> ⁷ for my mouth will utter truth;
>   wickedness is an abomination to my lips.
> ⁸ All the words of my mouth are righteous;
>   there is nothing twisted or crooked in them.
> ⁹ They are all straight to him who understands,
>   and right to those who find knowledge.
> ¹⁰ Take my instruction instead of silver,
>   and knowledge rather than choice gold,
> ¹¹ for wisdom is better than jewels,

LESSON 2:
WHAT ARE ELEMENTS OF HIS LOVE THAT WE WILL EXPEREINCE IF WE WALK WITH HIM?

> and all that you may desire cannot compare with her.
> [12] "I, wisdom, dwell with prudence,
>   and I find knowledge and discretion.
> [13] The fear of the LORD is hatred of evil.
> Pride and arrogance and the way of evil
>   and perverted speech I hate.
> [14] I have counsel and sound wisdom;
>   I have insight; I have strength.
> [15] By me kings reign,
>   and rulers decree what is just;
> [16] by me princes rule,
>   and nobles, all who govern justly.[a]
> [17] I love those who love me,
>   and those who seek me diligently find me.
> [18] Riches and honor are with me,
>   enduring wealth and righteousness.

_____
_____
_____
_____
_____

LESSON 2:
WHAT ARE ELEMENTS OF HIS LOVE THAT WE WILL EXPEREINCE IF WE WALK WITH HIM?

What are the elements of wisdom that we will be receiving? What do these mean for our everyday lives?

> **Read Isaiah 11:1–3:**
>
> The Righteous Reign of the Branch
> **11** There shall come forth a shoot from the stump of Jesse,
>   and a branch from his roots shall bear fruit.
> ² And the Spirit of the Lord shall rest upon him,
>   the Spirit of wisdom and understanding,
>   the Spirit of counsel and might,
>   the Spirit of knowledge and the fear of the LORD.
> ³ And his delight shall be in the fear of the LORD.
> He shall not judge by what his eyes see,
>   or decide disputes by what his ears hear,

_____
_____
_____
_____
_____

LESSON 2:
WHAT ARE ELEMENTS OF HIS LOVE THAT WE WILL EXPEREINCE IF WE WALK WITH HIM?

As God has us experience this beautiful, spiritual life, what is the main reason He demonstrates this to us? Why is this so important?

> **Read Isaiah 42:8–9:**
>
> [8] I am the LORD; that is my name;
> my glory I give to no other,
>   nor my praise to carved idols.
> [9] Behold, the former things have come to pass,
>   and new things I now declare;
> before they spring forth
>   I tell you of them."

_____
_____
_____
_____
_____

LESSON 3:
HOW DOES GOD'S LOVE LEAD US TO HIS GOOD, BEST AND SUPERNATURAL LIFE FOR US?

As a follower of Christ, where have we been raised? What does that mean for how we are to live? What does it mean that God has prepared good works for us to walk in? How are we then to understand how we walk with Him?

> **Read Ephesians 2:1–10:**
>
> By Grace Through Faith
> **2** And you were dead in the trespasses and sins ² in which you once walked, following the course of this world, following the prince of the power of the air, the spirit that is now at work in the sons of disobedience— ³ among whom we all once lived in the passions of our flesh, carrying out the desires of the body[a] and the mind, and were by nature children of wrath, like the rest of mankind.[b] ⁴ But[c] God, being rich in mercy, because of the great love with which he loved us, ⁵ even when we were dead in our trespasses, made us alive together with Christ—by grace you have been saved— ⁶ and raised us up with him and seated us with him in the heavenly places in Christ Jesus, ⁷ so that in the coming ages he might show the immeasurable riches of his grace in kindness toward us in Christ Jesus. ⁸ For by grace you have been saved through faith. And this is not your own doing; it is the gift of God, ⁹ not a result of works, so that no one may boast. ¹⁰ For we are his workmanship, created in Christ Jesus for good works, which God prepared beforehand, that we should walk in them.

> "He created us in His image to be the physical representation of the invisible God in a physical world."

_____
_____
_____
_____
_____

LESSON 3:
HOW DOES GOD'S LOVE LEAD US TO HIS GOOD, BEST AND SUPERNATURAL LIFE FOR US?

What is our role in discovering this life of "good" work that God has prepared? What does He then promise to give us? What does that mean?

> **Read Jeremiah 33:3:**
>
> ³ Call to me and I will answer you, and will tell you great and hidden things that you have not known.

_____
_____
_____
_____
_____

What does God promise as we receive His answers to our questions—things that only He knows? What is important for us to receive His answers and not be stubborn? Why?

> **Read Psalm 32:8–11:**
>
> ⁸ I will instruct you and teach you in the way you should go;
>   I will counsel you with my eye upon you.
> ⁹ Be not like a horse or a mule, without understanding,
>   which must be curbed with bit and bridle,
>   or it will not stay near you.
> ¹⁰ Many are the sorrows of the wicked,
>   but steadfast love surrounds the one who trusts in the Lord.
> ¹¹ Be glad in the LORD, and rejoice, O righteous,
>   and shout for joy, all you upright in heart!

_____
_____
_____
_____
_____

LESSON 3:
HOW DOES GOD'S LOVE LEAD US TO HIS GOOD, BEST AND SUPERNATURAL LIFE FOR US?

What is the role of the Holy Spirit? What does that mean? What will be the promised benefit to us? What does that mean for what we can expect in our difficult lives?

Read Romans 8:26–28:

8 I will instruct you and teach you in the way you should go;
   I will counsel you with my eye upon you.
²⁶ Be not like a horse or a mule, without understanding,
   which must be curbed with bit and bridle,
   or it will not stay near you.
²⁷ Many are the sorrows of the wicked,
   but steadfast love surrounds the one who trusts in the LORD.
²⁸ Be glad in the LORD, and rejoice, O righteous,
   and shout for joy, all you upright in heart!

_____
_____
_____
_____
_____

In order to experience the promised good from God, how are we to walk with Him and receive this good? What does that look like in our everyday lives?

Read Psalm 33:4–6; 10–12:

⁴ For the word of the LORD is upright,
   and all his work is done in faithfulness.
⁵ He loves righteousness and justice;
   the earth is full of the steadfast love of the LORD.
⁶ By the word of the LORD the heavens were made,
   and by the breath of his mouth all their host.
¹⁰ The Lord brings the counsel of the nations to nothing;
   he frustrates the plans of the peoples.

LESSON 3:
HOW DOES GOD'S LOVE LEAD US TO HIS GOOD, BEST AND SUPERNATURAL LIFE FOR US?

> [11] The counsel of the LORD stands forever,
>   the plans of his heart to all generations.
> [12] Blessed is the nation whose God is the LORD,
>   the people whom he has chosen as his heritage!

_____
_____
_____
_____
_____

What further does He promise as we walk with Him? What does this mean to how we live life?

> **Read Psalm 36:5–10:**
>
> [5] Your steadfast love, O LORD, extends to the heavens,
>   your faithfulness to the clouds.
> [6] Your righteousness is like the mountains of God;
>   your judgments are like the great deep;
>   man and beast you save, O LORD.
> [7] How precious is your steadfast love, O God!
>   The children of mankind take refuge in the shadow of your wings.
> [8] They feast on the abundance of your house,
>   and you give them drink from the river of your delights.
> [9] For with you is the fountain of life;
>   in your light do we see light.
> [10] Oh, continue your steadfast love to those who know you,
>   and your righteousness to the upright of heart!

_____
_____
_____
_____
_____

LESSON 3:
HOW DOES GOD'S LOVE LEAD US TO HIS GOOD, BEST AND SUPERNATURAL LIFE FOR US?

How does God deliver the Covenant to us? How does this demonstrate His love for us? Why is this so important for us?

> **Read Psalm 59:9–10; 16–17:**
>
> [9] O my Strength, I will watch for you,
>   for you, O God, are my fortress.
> [10] My God in his steadfast love[a] will meet me;
>   God will let me look in triumph on my enemies.
> [16] But I will sing of your strength;
>   I will sing aloud of your steadfast love in the morning.
> For you have been to me a fortress
>   and a refuge in the day of my distress.
> [17] O my Strength, I will sing praises to you,
>   for you, O God, are my fortress,
>   the God who shows me steadfast love.

_____
_____
_____
_____
_____

As we meet Him, what then will we experience? Why?

> **Read Psalm 21:3–7:**
>
> [3] For you meet him with rich blessings;
>   you set a crown of fine gold upon his head.
> [4] He asked life of you; you gave it to him,
>   length of days forever and ever.
> [5] His glory is great through your salvation;
>   splendor and majesty you bestow on him.
> [6] For you make him most blessed forever;[a]

LESSON 3:
HOW DOES GOD'S LOVE LEAD US TO HIS GOOD, BEST AND SUPERNATURAL LIFE FOR US?

> you make him glad with the joy of your presence.
> ⁷ For the king trusts in the LORD,
>   and through the steadfast love of the Most High he shall not be moved.

_____
_____
_____
_____
_____

In the following two sets of verses, what are other benefits of living in His presence? What does that then mean for what we will experience in our life? Why?

> **Read Psalm 84:9–12:**
>
> ⁹ Behold our shield, O God;
>   look on the face of your anointed!
> ¹⁰ For a day in your courts is better
>   than a thousand elsewhere.
> I would rather be a doorkeeper in the house of my God
>   than dwell in the tents of wickedness.
> ¹¹ For the LORD God is a sun and shield;
>   the LORD bestows favor and honor.
> No good thing does he withhold
>   from those who walk uprightly.
> ¹² O LORD of hosts,
>   blessed is the one who trusts in you!

_____
_____
_____
_____
_____

LESSON 3:
HOW DOES GOD'S LOVE LEAD US TO HIS GOOD, BEST AND SUPERNATURAL LIFE FOR US?

> **Read Psalm 85:10–13:**
>
> [10] Steadfast love and faithfulness meet;
>   righteousness and peace kiss each other.
> [11] Faithfulness springs up from the ground,
>   and righteousness looks down from the sky.
> [12] Yes, the LORD will give what is good,
>   and our land will yield its increase.
> [13] Righteousness will go before him
>   and make his footsteps a way.

_____

_____

_____

_____

From the following two sets of verses: To receive His good things, what does God promise regarding the difficult things in our lives? What does this practically mean? What then shall we expect on how to face these difficulties?

> **Read Isaiah 45:1–6:**
>
> Cyrus, God's Instrument
> **45** Thus says the LORD to his anointed, to Cyrus,
>   whose right hand I have grasped,
> to subdue nations before him
>   and to loose the belts of kings,
> to open doors before him
>   that gates may not be closed:
> [2] "I will go before you
>   and level the exalted places,[a]
> I will break in pieces the doors of bronze
>   and cut through the bars of iron,
> [3] I will give you the treasures of darkness
>   and the hoards in secret places,

LESSON 3:
HOW DOES GOD'S LOVE LEAD US TO HIS GOOD, BEST AND SUPERNATURAL LIFE FOR US?

> that you may know that it is I, the LORD,
>   the God of Israel, who call you by your name.
> [4] For the sake of my servant Jacob,
>   and Israel my chosen,
> I call you by your name,
>   I name you, though you do not know me.
> [5] I am the Lord, and there is no other,
>   besides me there is no God;
>   I equip you, though you do not know me,
> [6] that people may know, from the rising of the sun
>   and from the west, that there is none besides me;
>   I am the LORD, and there is no other.

_____
_____
_____
_____
_____

Read Isaiah 42:16:

> [16] And I will lead the blind
>   in a way that they do not know,
> in paths that they have not known
>   I will guide them.
> I will turn the darkness before them into light,
>   the rough places into level ground.
> These are the things I do,
>   and I do not forsake them.

_____
_____
_____
_____
_____

LESSON 3:
HOW DOES GOD'S LOVE LEAD US TO HIS GOOD, BEST AND SUPERNATURAL LIFE FOR US?

How does God bring this exceptional life to us? What is important for how we are to process and receive His solutions? What does that look like as we learn how to process in this way?

Read Jeremiah 32:37–42; Ephesians 4:1–6:

37 Behold, I will gather them from all the countries to which I drove them in my anger and my wrath and in great indignation. I will bring them back to this place, and I will make them dwell in safety. 38 And they shall be my people, and I will be their God. 39 I will give them one heart and one way, that they may fear me forever, for their own good and the good of their children after them. 40 I will make with them an everlasting covenant, that I will not turn away from doing good to them. And I will put the fear of me in their hearts, that they may not turn from me. 41 I will rejoice in doing them good, and I will plant them in this land in faithfulness, with all my heart and all my soul.

42 "For thus says the Lord: Just as I have brought all this great disaster upon this people, so I will bring upon them all the good that I promise them.

Unity in the Body of Christ
4 I therefore, a prisoner for the Lord, urge you to walk in a manner worthy of the calling to which you have been called, 2 with all humility and gentleness, with patience, bearing with one another in love, 3 eager to maintain the unity of the Spirit in the bond of peace. 4 There is one body and one Spirit—just as you were called to the one hope that belongs to your call— 5 one Lord, one faith, one baptism, 6 one God and Father of all, who is over all and through all and in all.

_____
_____
_____
_____
_____

LESSON 3:
HOW DOES GOD'S LOVE LEAD US TO HIS GOOD, BEST AND SUPERNATURAL LIFE FOR US?

From the following two sets of verses, what is important for us to pursue? What does that mean? How are we to pursue this?

> **Read Zechariah 8:18–19:**
>
> [18] And the word of the Lord of hosts came to me, saying, [19] "Thus says the Lord of hosts: The fast of the fourth month and the fast of the fifth and the fast of the seventh and the fast of the tenth shall be to the house of Judah seasons of joy and gladness and cheerful feasts. Therefore love truth and peace.

_____
_____
_____
_____
_____

> **Read John 3:19–21:**
>
> [19] And this is the judgment: the light has come into the world, and people loved the darkness rather than the light because their works were evil. [20] For everyone who does wicked things hates the light and does not come to the light, lest his works should be exposed. [21] But whoever does what is true comes to the light, so that it may be clearly seen that his works have been carried out in God."

_____
_____
_____
_____
_____

LESSON 3:
HOW DOES GOD'S LOVE LEAD US TO HIS GOOD, BEST AND SUPERNATURAL LIFE FOR US?

As we receive truth, how does God give us an indication that we are receiving truth versus not receiving truth? How does this work for us? Why is this so significant for us?

> **Read 1 John 3:19–24:**
>
> [19] By this we shall know that we are of the truth and reassure our heart before him; [20] for whenever our heart condemns us, God is greater than our heart, and he knows everything. [21] Beloved, if our heart does not condemn us, we have confidence before God; [22] and whatever we ask we receive from him, because we keep his commandments and do what pleases him. [23] And this is his commandment, that we believe in the name of his Son Jesus Christ and love one another, just as he has commanded us. [24] Whoever keeps his commandments abides in God,[a] and God[b] in him. And by this we know that he abides in us, by the Spirit whom he has given us.

_____
_____
_____
_____
_____

LESSON 3:
HOW DOES GOD'S LOVE LEAD US TO HIS GOOD, BEST AND SUPERNATURAL LIFE FOR US?

How can we have assurance that we are learning truth and following God's will for us? What then are we to expect to receive, and how are we to follow?

Read John 14:15–24:

Jesus Promises the Holy Spirit

[15] "If you love me, you will keep my commandments. [16] And I will ask the Father, and he will give you another Helper,[a] to be with you forever, [17] even the Spirit of truth, whom the world cannot receive, because it neither sees him nor knows him. You know him, for he dwells with you and will be[b] in you.

[18] "I will not leave you as orphans; I will come to you. [19] Yet a little while and the world will see me no more, but you will see me. Because I live, you also will live. [20] In that day you will know that I am in my Father, and you in me, and I in you. [21] Whoever has my commandments and keeps them, he it is who loves me. And he who loves me will be loved by my Father, and I will love him and manifest myself to him." [22] Judas (not Iscariot) said to him, "Lord, how is it that you will manifest yourself to us, and not to the world?" [23] Jesus answered him, "If anyone loves me, he will keep my word, and my Father will love him, and we will come to him and make our home with him. [24] Whoever does not love me does not keep my words. And the word that you hear is not mine but the Father's who sent me.

_____
_____
_____
_____
_____

LESSON 3:
HOW DOES GOD'S LOVE LEAD US TO HIS GOOD, BEST AND SUPERNATURAL LIFE FOR US?

What does it mean that God establishes every good for us? How might we then receive this as we face difficulties and trouble? What does that mean we can expect as outcomes of these difficulties and troubles?

> **Read 2 Thessalonians 2:16–17:**
>
> [16] Now may our Lord Jesus Christ himself, and God our Father, who loved us and gave us eternal comfort and good hope through grace, [17] comfort your hearts and establish them in every good work and word.

_____

_____

_____

_____

As God meets us and gives us hope, what does He wish to give us? Why is this so significant to how we live and receive His good work?

> **Read Psalm 21:1–7:**
>
> The King Rejoices in the Lord's Strength
> To the choirmaster. A Psalm of David.
> **21** O LORD, in your strength the king rejoices,
>   and in your salvation how greatly he exults!
> [2] You have given him his heart's desire
>   and have not withheld the request of his lips. _Selah_
> [3] For you meet him with rich blessings;
>   you set a crown of fine gold upon his head.
> [4] He asked life of you; you gave it to him,
>   length of days forever and ever.
> [5] His glory is great through your salvation;
>   splendor and majesty you bestow on him.

LESSON 3:
HOW DOES GOD'S LOVE LEAD US TO HIS GOOD, BEST AND SUPERNATURAL LIFE FOR US?

> [6] For you make him most blessed forever;[a]
>   you make him glad with the joy of your presence.
> [7] For the king trusts in the LORD,
>   and through the steadfast love of the Most High he shall not be moved.

_____
_____
_____
_____
_____

As a disciple of Christ, what are we to learn? What is the significance of this for how we then follow Him?

> **Read Matthew 28:18–20:**
>
> [18] And Jesus came and said to them, "All authority in heaven and on earth has been given to me. [19] Go therefore and make disciples of all nations, baptizing them in[a] the name of the Father and of the Son and of the Holy Spirit, [20] teaching them to observe all that I have commanded you. And behold, I am with you always, to the end of the age."

_____
_____
_____
_____
_____

LESSON 3:
HOW DOES GOD'S LOVE LEAD US TO HIS GOOD, BEST AND SUPERNATURAL LIFE FOR US?

Whose race are we to run? What is important as we run this race? What does that mean for how we then run our race?

> **Read Hebrews 12:1–2:**
>
> Jesus, Founder and Perfecter of Our Faith
> **12** Therefore, since we are surrounded by so great a cloud of witnesses, let us also lay aside every weight, and sin which clings so closely, and let us run with endurance the race that is set before us, ² looking to Jesus, the founder and perfecter of our faith, who for the joy that was set before him endured the cross, despising the shame, and is seated at the right hand of the throne of God.

_____
_____
_____
_____
_____

LESSON 4: WHAT ARE THE CONDITIONS OF LIVING IN AND RECEIVING GOD'S LOVE THAT PROVIDES WONDERFUL ASPECTS OF THE FULLNESS OF GOD'S LIFE?

What does God set before us? What is the reason, and what are the consequences for the choice we make? How does God wish us to respond? What are the benefits of choosing so? Why is this so important for us to experience His love?

Read Deuteronomy 30:11–20:

The Choice of Life and Death

[11] "For this commandment that I command you today is not too hard for you, neither is it far off. [12] It is not in heaven, that you should say, 'Who will ascend to heaven for us and bring it to us, that we may hear it and do it?' [13] Neither is it beyond the sea, that you should say, 'Who will go over the sea for us and bring it to us, that we may hear it and do it?' [14] But the word is very near you. It is in your mouth and in your heart, so that you can do it.

[15] "See, I have set before you today life and good, death and evil. [16] If you obey the commandments of the Lord your God[a] that I command you today, by loving the LORD your God, by walking in his ways, and by keeping his commandments and his statutes and his rules,[b] then you shall live and multiply, and the LORD your God will bless you in the land that you are entering to take possession of it. [17] But if your heart turns away, and you will not hear, but are drawn away to worship other gods and serve them, [18] I declare to you today, that you shall surely perish. You shall not live long in the land that you are going over the Jordan to enter and possess. [19] I call heaven and earth to witness against you today, that I have set before you life and death, blessing and curse. Therefore choose life, that you and your offspring may live, [20] loving the LORD your God, obeying his voice and holding fast to him, for he is your life and length of days, that you may dwell in the land that the Lord swore to your fathers, to Abraham, to Isaac, and to Jacob, to give them."

> **"We're not forced to receive His love, but have the choice to receive this love and then remain in the intimacy of this love."**

LESSON 4: WHAT ARE THE CONDITIONS OF LIVING IN AND RECEIVING GOD'S LOVE THAT PROVIDES WONDERFUL ASPECTS OF THE FULLNESS OF GOD'S LIFE?

_____
_____
_____
_____
_____

How does choosing Him mean we are loving Him? What is His heart toward you, and why does choosing Him thrill His heart?

> **Read Deuteronomy 6:4–5:**
>
> [4] "Hear, O Israel: The LORD our God, the Lord is one.[a] [5] You shall love the LORD your God with all your heart and with all your soul and with all your might.

_____
_____
_____
_____
_____

LESSON 4: WHAT ARE THE CONDITIONS OF LIVING IN AND RECEIVING GOD'S LOVE THAT PROVIDES WONDERFUL ASPECTS OF THE FULLNESS OF GOD'S LIFE?

How does Jesus define love here? How does that differ from most Christians' understanding of love? How then shall we respond to experience God's love and for us to love Him?

Read Luke 11:37–12:3:

Woes to the Pharisees and Lawyers

37 While Jesus[a] was speaking, a Pharisee asked him to dine with him, so he went in and reclined at table. 38 The Pharisee was astonished to see that he did not first wash before dinner. 39 And the Lord said to him, "Now you Pharisees cleanse the outside of the cup and of the dish, but inside you are full of greed and wickedness. 40 You fools! Did not he who made the outside make the inside also? 41 But give as alms those things that are within, and behold, everything is clean for you.

42 "But woe to you Pharisees! For you tithe mint and rue and every herb, and neglect justice and the love of God. These you ought to have done, without neglecting the others. 43 Woe to you Pharisees! For you love the best seat in the synagogues and greetings in the marketplaces. 44 Woe to you! For you are like unmarked graves, and people walk over them without knowing it."

45 One of the lawyers answered him, "Teacher, in saying these things you insult us also." 46 And he said, "Woe to you lawyers also! For you load people with burdens hard to bear, and you yourselves do not touch the burdens with one of your fingers. 47 Woe to you! For you build the tombs of the prophets whom your fathers killed. 48 So you are witnesses and you consent to the deeds of your fathers, for they killed them, and you build their tombs. 49 Therefore also the Wisdom of God said, 'I will send them prophets and apostles, some of whom they will kill and persecute,' 50 so that the blood of all the prophets, shed from the foundation of the world, may be charged against this generation, 51 from the blood of Abel to the blood of Zechariah, who perished between the altar and the sanctuary. Yes, I tell you, it will be required of this generation. 52 Woe to you lawyers! For you have taken away the key of knowledge. You did not enter yourselves, and you hindered those who were entering."

53 As he went away from there, the scribes and the Pharisees began to press him hard and to provoke him to speak about many things, 54 lying in wait for him, to catch him in something he might say.

LESSON 4: WHAT ARE THE CONDITIONS OF LIVING IN AND RECEIVING GOD'S LOVE THAT PROVIDES WONDERFUL ASPECTS OF THE FULLNESS OF GOD'S LIFE?

> **Beware of the Leaven of the Pharisees**
> **12** In the meantime, when so many thousands of the people had gathered together that they were trampling one another, he began to say to his disciples first, "Beware of the leaven of the Pharisees, which is hypocrisy. **2** Nothing is covered up that will not be revealed, or hidden that will not be known. **3** Therefore whatever you have said in the dark shall be heard in the light, and what you have whispered in private rooms shall be proclaimed on the housetops.

_____
_____
_____
_____
_____

What is required of us to receive the Covenant life—the super-abundant blessed life? What do all these mean regarding how we love Him? How do we fulfill these?

> **Read Deuteronomy 10:12–13:**
>
> **Circumcise Your Heart**
> **12** "And now, Israel, what does the LORD your God require of you, but to fear the LORD your God, to walk in all his ways, to love him, to serve the LORD your God with all your heart and with all your soul, **13** and to keep the commandments and statutes of the LORD, which I am commanding you today for your good?

_____
_____
_____
_____
_____

LESSON 4: WHAT ARE THE CONDITIONS OF LIVING IN AND RECEIVING GOD'S LOVE THAT PROVIDES WONDERFUL ASPECTS OF THE FULLNESS OF GOD'S LIFE?

As we walk with Him, what is our privilege? How does this stimulate Him giving us love, and us loving Him back? What is the reason for this privilege?

> **Read Ephesians 3:12:**
>
> ¹² in whom we have boldness and access with confidence through our faith in him.

_____

_____

_____

_____

_____

As we love Him with all our heart, mind, and soul, what do we find our delight in? What does this mean, and why is this so important to demonstrate our love?

> **Read Psalm 119:41–48:**
>
> Waw
> ⁴¹ Let your steadfast love come to me, O LORD,
>   your salvation according to your promise;
> ⁴² then shall I have an answer for him who taunts me,
>   for I trust in your word.
> ⁴³ And take not the word of truth utterly out of my mouth,
>   for my hope is in your rules.
> ⁴⁴ I will keep your law continually,
>   forever and ever,
> ⁴⁵ and I shall walk in a wide place,
>   for I have sought your precepts.
> ⁴⁶ I will also speak of your testimonies before kings
>   and shall not be put to shame,

LESSON 4: WHAT ARE THE CONDITIONS OF LIVING IN AND RECEIVING GOD'S LOVE THAT PROVIDES WONDERFUL ASPECTS OF THE FULLNESS OF GOD'S LIFE?

> ^{47} for I find my delight in your commandments,
>   which I love.
> ^{48} I will lift up my hands toward your commandments, which I love,
>   and I will meditate on your statutes.

___

As we seek His instruction to demonstrate our love, what are we to pursue? How do we receive truth? What does this mean to how we process with Him? Why?

> **Read John 18:37–38:**
>
> ^{37} Then Pilate said to him, "So you are a king?" Jesus answered, "You say that I am a king. For this purpose I was born and for this purpose I have come into the world—to bear witness to the truth. Everyone who is of the truth listens to my voice." ^{38} Pilate said to him, "What is truth?"
>
> After he had said this, he went back outside to the Jews and told them, "I find no guilt in him.

___

LESSON 4: WHAT ARE THE CONDITIONS OF LIVING IN AND RECEIVING GOD'S LOVE THAT PROVIDES WONDERFUL ASPECTS OF THE FULLNESS OF GOD'S LIFE?

From the following two sets of verses, what do we need to be careful of? How are we to understand the difference between truth and false? Why is this so important in our experience of God's love?

Read Deuteronomy 13:1–4:

13 "If a prophet or a dreamer of dreams arises among you and gives you a sign or a wonder, ² and the sign or wonder that he tells you comes to pass, and if he says, 'Let us go after other gods,' which you have not known, 'and let us serve them,' ³ you shall not listen to the words of that prophet or that dreamer of dreams. For the Lord your God is testing you, to know whether you love the Lord your God with all your heart and with all your soul. ⁴ You shall walk after the Lord your God and fear him and keep his commandments and obey his voice, and you shall serve him and hold fast to him.

_____
_____
_____
_____
_____

Read 1 John 4:1–6:

Test the Spirits
4 Beloved, do not believe every spirit, but test the spirits to see whether they are from God, for many false prophets have gone out into the world. ² By this you know the Spirit of God: every spirit that confesses that Jesus Christ has come in the flesh is from God, ³ and every spirit that does not confess Jesus is not from God. This is the spirit of the antichrist, which you heard was coming and now is in the world already. ⁴ Little children, you are from God and have overcome them, for he who is in you is greater than he who is in the world. ⁵ They are from the world; therefore they speak from the world, and the world listens to them. ⁶ We are from God. Whoever knows God listens to us; whoever is not from God does not listen to us. By this we know the Spirit of truth and the spirit of error.

LESSON 4: WHAT ARE THE CONDITIONS OF LIVING IN AND RECEIVING GOD'S LOVE THAT PROVIDES WONDERFUL ASPECTS OF THE FULLNESS OF GOD'S LIFE?

_____
_____
_____
_____
_____

As we further understand delighting in His instruction, what does that lead us to? What does that mean for how we live? In what way does this characterize what is said about you? Why?

> **Read Psalm 40:6–10:**
>
> ⁶ In sacrifice and offering you have not delighted,
>   but you have given me an open ear.[a]
> Burnt offering and sin offering
>   you have not required.
> ⁷ Then I said, "Behold, I have come;
>   in the scroll of the book it is written of me:
> ⁸ I delight to do your will, O my God;
>   your law is within my heart."
> ⁹ I have told the glad news of deliverance[b]
>   in the great congregation;
> behold, I have not restrained my lips,
>   as you know, O LORD.
> ¹⁰ I have not hidden your deliverance within my heart;
>   I have spoken of your faithfulness and your salvation;
> I have not concealed your steadfast love and your faithfulness
>   from the great congregation.

_____
_____
_____
_____
_____

LESSON 4: WHAT ARE THE CONDITIONS OF LIVING IN AND RECEIVING GOD'S LOVE THAT PROVIDES WONDERFUL ASPECTS OF THE FULLNESS OF GOD'S LIFE?

As we pursue love, what else are we to pursue? How do you define this? What does this look like as we engaged with others in our personal community—spouse, family, friends, small group? Why is this such a special privilege?

> **Read 1 Corinthians 14:1–3:**
>
> Prophecy and Tongues
> **14** Pursue love, and earnestly desire the spiritual gifts, especially that you may prophesy. ² For one who speaks in a tongue speaks not to men but to God; for no one understands him, but he utters mysteries in the Spirit. ³ On the other hand, the one who prophesies speaks to people for their upbuilding and encouragement and consolation.

_____
_____
_____
_____
_____

As we experience God's love, what does He promise? What does that mean? Why is this so significant as we face difficulties and life's troubles?

> **Read Proverbs 25:12–15:**
>
> ¹² Like a gold ring or an ornament of gold
>   is a wise reprover to a listening ear.
> ¹³ Like the cold of snow in the time of harvest
>   is a faithful messenger to those who send him;
>   he refreshes the soul of his masters.
> ¹⁴ Like clouds and wind without rain
>   is a man who boasts of a gift he does not give.
> ¹⁵ With patience a ruler may be persuaded,
>   and a soft tongue will break a bone.

LESSON 4: WHAT ARE THE CONDITIONS OF LIVING IN AND RECEIVING GOD'S LOVE THAT PROVIDES WONDERFUL ASPECTS OF THE FULLNESS OF GOD'S LIFE?

_____
_____
_____
_____
_____

Knowing that He will deliver the Covenant because of His love for us, what is important in order for us to receive it? What does that mean? Why is this such a critical part of the process?

> **Read Psalm 27:13–14:**
>
> [13] I believe that I shall look[a] upon the goodness of the LORD
>   in the land of the living!
> [14] Wait for the LORD;
>   be strong, and let your heart take courage;
>   wait for the LORD!

_____
_____
_____
_____
_____
_____

LESSON 5:
HOW DO WE LOVE OTHERS AND HELP THEM TO LEARN TO LOVE GOD WITH ALL THEIR HEART?

As we are having a heart to love others—a significant part of our commands from Christ—what is necessary for us to be able to truly love others? What does that mean? Why is this so important to the process of us fulfilling His command to love others?

Read 1 John 5:1–3:

Overcoming the World
5 Everyone who believes that Jesus is the Christ has been born of God, and everyone who loves the Father loves whoever has been born of him. ² By this we know that we love the children of God, when we love God and obey his commandments. ³ For this is the love of God, that we keep his commandments. And his commandments are not burdensome.

"We're not forced to receive His love, but have the choice to receive this love and then remain in the intimacy of this love."

_____
_____
_____
_____
_____

LESSON 5:
HOW DO WE LOVE OTHERS AND HELP THEM TO LEARN TO LOVE GOD WITH ALL THEIR HEART?

As we consider loving others, list the known elements of what it means to have our heart and actions toward others? How do we fulfill this? Why is this list so important to how we live this out?

> **Read Leviticus 19:10–18:**
>
> [10] And you shall not strip your vineyard bare, neither shall you gather the fallen grapes of your vineyard. You shall leave them for the poor and for the sojourner: I am the LORD your God.
>
> [11] "You shall not steal; you shall not deal falsely; you shall not lie to one another. [12] You shall not swear by my name falsely, and so profane the name of your God: I am the LORD.
>
> [13] "You shall not oppress your neighbor or rob him. The wages of a hired worker shall not remain with you all night until the morning. [14] You shall not curse the deaf or put a stumbling block before the blind, but you shall fear your God: I am the LORD.
>
> [15] "You shall do no injustice in court. You shall not be partial to the poor or defer to the great, but in righteousness shall you judge your neighbor. [16] You shall not go around as a slanderer among your people, and you shall not stand up against the life[a] of your neighbor: I am the LORD.
>
> [17] "You shall not hate your brother in your heart, but you shall reason frankly with your neighbor, lest you incur sin because of him. [18] You shall not take vengeance or bear a grudge against the sons of your own people, but you shall love your neighbor as yourself: I am the LORD.

_____
_____
_____
_____
_____

LESSON 5:
HOW DO WE LOVE OTHERS AND HELP THEM TO LEARN TO LOVE GOD WITH ALL THEIR HEART?

As we carry out love, what are the characteristics that we are to experience that we then can offer to others? What does this look like in our practical lives? How does this demonstrate that we are loving others?

> **Read 1 Corinthians 13:1–13:**
>
> The Way of Love
> **13** If I speak in the tongues of men and of angels, but have not love, I am a noisy gong or a clanging cymbal. ² And if I have prophetic powers, and understand all mysteries and all knowledge, and if I have all faith, so as to remove mountains, but have not love, I am nothing. ³ If I give away all I have, and if I deliver up my body to be burned,[a] but have not love, I gain nothing.
>
> ⁴ Love is patient and kind; love does not envy or boast; it is not arrogant ⁵ or rude. It does not insist on its own way; it is not irritable or resentful;[b] ⁶ it does not rejoice at wrongdoing, but rejoices with the truth. ⁷ Love bears all things, believes all things, hopes all things, endures all things.
>
> ⁸ Love never ends. As for prophecies, they will pass away; as for tongues, they will cease; as for knowledge, it will pass away. ⁹ For we know in part and we prophesy in part, ¹⁰ but when the perfect comes, the partial will pass away. ¹¹ When I was a child, I spoke like a child, I thought like a child, I reasoned like a child. When I became a man, I gave up childish ways. ¹² For now we see in a mirror dimly, but then face to face. Now I know in part; then I shall know fully, even as I have been fully known.
>
> ¹³ So now faith, hope, and love abide, these three; but the greatest of these is love.

_____
_____
_____
_____
_____

LESSON 5:
HOW DO WE LOVE OTHERS AND HELP THEM TO LEARN TO LOVE GOD WITH ALL THEIR HEART?

What is the purpose of being called to love others? How do we fulfill this in practical ways? What does that mean as to how we are then to live?

> **Read 1 Corinthians 12:1–11:**
>
> Spiritual Gifts
> **12** Now concerning[a] spiritual gifts,[b] brothers,[c] I do not want you to be uninformed. ² You know that when you were pagans you were led astray to mute idols, however you were led. ³ Therefore I want you to understand that no one speaking in the Spirit of God ever says "Jesus is accursed!" and no one can say "Jesus is Lord" except in the Holy Spirit.
>
> ⁴ Now there are varieties of gifts, but the same Spirit; ⁵ and there are varieties of service, but the same Lord; 6 and there are varieties of activities, but it is the same God who empowers them all in everyone. ⁷ To each is given the manifestation of the Spirit for the common good. ⁸ For to one is given through the Spirit the utterance of wisdom, and to another the utterance of knowledge according to the same Spirit, ⁹ to another faith by the same Spirit, to another gifts of healing by the one Spirit, ¹⁰ to another the working of miracles, to another prophecy, to another the ability to distinguish between spirits, to another various kinds of tongues, to another the interpretation of tongues. ¹¹ All these are empowered by one and the same Spirit, who apportions to each one individually as he wills.

_____
_____
_____
_____
_____

LESSON 5:
HOW DO WE LOVE OTHERS AND HELP THEM TO LEARN TO LOVE GOD WITH ALL THEIR HEART?

How do I make sure I do not neglect loving others by doing good? What does that mean then for how I do good? Why is this so important?

> **Read Hebrews 13:16:**
>
> [16] Do not neglect to do good and to share what you have, for such sacrifices are pleasing to God.

_____
_____
_____
_____
_____

Since loving others means more than just doing things, what is important for us to truly love others? What does this mean for us? Why is this so important?

> **Read Micah 6:8:**
>
> [8] He has told you, O man, what is good;
>   and what does the Lord require of you
> but to do justice, and to love kindness,[a]
>   and to walk humbly with your God?

_____
_____
_____
_____
_____

LESSON 5:
HOW DO WE LOVE OTHERS AND HELP THEM TO LEARN TO LOVE GOD WITH ALL THEIR HEART?

God calls us to pass love along by our priority of what? What does this look like in practical ways in our lives? Why is this such an important element of love?

> **Read 2 Timothy 2:1–2:**
>
> A Good Soldier of Christ Jesus
> **2** You then, my child, be strengthened by the grace that is in Christ Jesus, ² and what you have heard from me in the presence of many witnesses entrust to faithful men,[a] who will be able to teach others also.

_____
_____
_____
_____
_____

As an important element of loving others, what is one of our roles? What does an ambassador do? How is this carried out? What does that mean for how we serve in this way?

> **Read 2 Corinthians 5:13–20:**
>
> ¹³ For if we are beside ourselves, it is for God; if we are in our right mind, it is for you. ¹⁴ For the love of Christ controls us, because we have concluded this: that one has died for all, therefore all have died; ¹⁵ and he died for all, that those who live might no longer live for themselves but for him who for their sake died and was raised.
>
> ¹⁶ From now on, therefore, we regard no one according to the flesh. Even though we once regarded Christ according to the flesh, we regard him thus no longer. ¹⁷ Therefore, if anyone is in Christ, he is a new creation. [a] The old has passed away; behold, the new has come. ¹⁸ All this is from God, who through Christ reconciled us to himself and gave us the ministry of reconciliation; ¹⁹ that is, in Christ God was reconciling[b] the world to himself, not

LESSON 5:
HOW DO WE LOVE OTHERS AND HELP THEM TO LEARN TO LOVE GOD WITH ALL THEIR HEART?

> counting their trespasses against them, and entrusting to us the message of reconciliation. [20] Therefore, we are ambassadors for Christ, God making his appeal through us. We implore you on behalf of Christ, be reconciled to God.

_____
_____
_____
_____
_____

What is God's purpose in our loving others? Why? How do we then participate in this?

> **Read 2 Corinthians 13:11:**
>
> Final Greetings
> [11] Finally, brothers,[a] rejoice. Aim for restoration, comfort one another,[b] agree with one another, live in peace; and the God of love and peace will be with you.

_____
_____
_____
_____
_____

LESSON 5:
HOW DO WE LOVE OTHERS AND HELP THEM TO LEARN TO LOVE GOD WITH ALL THEIR HEART?

Others who we are called to love—including ourselves—are burdened and heavy laden. How do we love others to release these burdens and heaviness? What does that mean for the process into which we are called to love others? Why?

> **Read Matthew 11:28–30:**
>
> 28 Come to me, all who labor and are heavy laden, and I will give you rest. 29 Take my yoke upon you, and learn from me, for I am gentle and lowly in heart, and you will find rest for your souls. 30 For my yoke is easy, and my burden is light."

_____
_____
_____
_____

One element of life is hurt and anger regarding how people are treated, which is a primary ingredient to burden and heaviness. How do we understand and receive forgiveness? Why is this so important to releasing the burden and heaviness?

> **Read Romans 8:1–2:**
>
> Life in the Spirit
> **8** There is therefore now no condemnation for those who are in Christ Jesus.[a] 2 For the law of the Spirit of life has set you[b] free in Christ Jesus from the law of sin and death.

_____
_____
_____
_____
_____

LESSON 5:
HOW DO WE LOVE OTHERS AND HELP THEM TO LEARN TO LOVE GOD WITH ALL THEIR HEART?

As we process our anger and hurt because of what others have done to or against us, what is important to how we address this process? What does that mean for us and how we carry this out? Why is that so important for us in this process?

> **Read Ephesians 4:25–26:**
>
> ²⁵ Therefore, having put away falsehood, let each one of you speak the truth with his neighbor, for we are members one of another. ²⁶ Be angry and do not sin; do not let the sun go down on your anger,

_____
_____
_____
_____
_____

How are we to handle people who have angered, hurt, or opposed us who are not willing to process truth—and basically do not care? What is important for us in releasing the burden of this difficult relationship? Why is this so critical in our ability to carry out God's love?

> **Read Romans 12:9–20:**
>
> Marks of the True Christian
> ⁹ Let love be genuine. Abhor what is evil; hold fast to what is good. ¹⁰ Love one another with brotherly affection. Outdo one another in showing honor. ¹¹ Do not be slothful in zeal, be fervent in spirit,[a] serve the Lord. ¹² Rejoice in hope, be patient in tribulation, be constant in prayer. ¹³ Contribute to the needs of the saints and seek to show hospitality.
>
> ¹⁴ Bless those who persecute you; bless and do not curse them. ¹⁵ Rejoice with those who rejoice, weep with those who weep. ¹⁶ Live in harmony with one another. Do not be haughty, but associate with the lowly.[b] Never be wise in your own sight. ¹⁷ Repay no one evil for evil, but give thought to do what

LESSON 5:
HOW DO WE LOVE OTHERS AND HELP THEM TO LEARN TO LOVE GOD WITH ALL THEIR HEART?

> is honorable in the sight of all. [18] If possible, so far as it depends on you, live peaceably with all. [19] Beloved, never avenge yourselves, but leave it[c] to the wrath of God, for it is written, "Vengeance is mine, I will repay, says the Lord." [20] To the contrary, "if your enemy is hungry, feed him; if he is thirsty, give him something to drink; for by so doing you will heap burning coals on his head."

_____
_____
_____
_____
_____

www.ingramcontent.com/pod-product-compliance
Lightning Source LLC
LaVergne TN
LVHW071658060526
838201LV00037B/372